SPACE

GALAXIES
AND
STARS

IAN GRAHAM

A⁺
Smart Apple Media

Published by Smart Apple Media,
an imprint of Black Rabbit Books
P.O. Box 3263, Mankato, Minnesota, 56002
www.blackrabbitbooks.com

Designed by Guy Callaby
Edited by Mary-Jane Wilkins

Cataloging-in-Publication Data is available
from the Library of Congress

ISBN 978-1-62588-208-0

Picture acknowledgements
t = top, b = bottom, l = left, r = right
page 1 Wolfgang Kloehr; 2-3 inigo cia;
4 pixelparticle; 5 Maria Starovoytova;
6 Catmando; 7, 8 a. v. ley; 9 Lionel
Alvergnas/all Shutterstock; 10 Image
Work/amanaimagesRF/Thinkstock;
11 peresanz; 12 Viktar Malyshchyts;
13 Vadim Sadovski/all Shutterstock;
14 ESO/NASA/JPL-Caltech/M.
Kornmesser/R. Hurt/ http://www.eso.
org/public/images/eso1339a; 15 Nick
Risinger/ http://commons.wikimedia.org/
wiki/File:Milky_Way_Galaxy.jpg;
16 peresanz; 17 a. v. ley; 18-19 Henner
Damke/all Shutterstock; 19t Stocktrek
Images/Thinkstock; 20 LingHK; 21 jupeart/
both Shutterstock
Cover Vadim Sadovski, Giovanni
Benintende/Shutterstock

Printed in China

DAD0057
032014
9 8 7 6 5 4 3 2 1

CONTENTS

THE NIGHT SKY

At night, the sky is full of twinkling points of light. Most of them are stars like the Sun. They look smaller than the Sun because they are further away.

RISING AND SETTING

Every night, the stars rise in the east, cross the sky and set in the west. They seem to move like this because the Earth is spinning.

On a clear night, you can see about 2,000 stars.

Galaxies

Stars are not spread out evenly in the Universe. They travel through space in giant groups called galaxies. Each galaxy has billions of stars and there are billions of galaxies.

Stars travel through space together in galaxies like this.

LIGHT YEARS

The distances between stars are so big that they are measured in light years. A light year is the distance light travels in one year —six trillion miles (ten trillion km).

SPOTLIGHT ON SPACE

HOW STARS BEGIN

Stars form in vast clouds of gas and dust called nebulae. New stars are still forming today far away in space.

MAKING STARS

Inside a nebula, the gas is thicker in some places. These thicker clumps of gas pull more gas toward them. They grow into bigger balls of gas and they heat up.

New stars are forming in this cloud of gas called the Eagle Nebula.

SWITCHING ON

When a ball of gas is massive enough and its core is hot enough, it bursts into light as a new star. One giant cloud of gas can make lots of stars.

STARTING STARBIRTH

Starbirth can be set off when an old star explodes. If the blast pushes against a nearby cloud of gas, it squashes parts of the cloud and begins to form new stars.

The brightest stars here, sparkling like jewels, are new young stars.

Star colors

Apart from the Sun, stars look like twinkling pinpoints of light. And they all look the same, although they are not all the same. Some stars are much hotter than others.

Hot and hotter

You can tell how hot a star is by its color. The hottest stars are blue. The coolest are red. The Sun is a yellow star.

The Pleiades is a group of hot blue stars.

Imagine what it would be like to have two Suns in the sky!

STAR TWINS

Sometimes, two stars are so close together that they circle around each other. A pair of stars together like this are called a binary star.

TURNING UP THE BRIGHTNESS

Some stars change in brightness. They grow brighter and dimmer, then brighter again. They are called variable stars. Scientists have recorded tens of thousands of them.

SPOTLIGHT ON SPACE

CONSTELLATIONS

Stargazers divide the sky into groups of stars called constellations. They use the constellations to help them find their way around the sky.

PICKING NAMES

Thousands of years ago, constellations were named after the people and animals in myths and legends. We still use some of these ancient names for constellations today.

THE ZODIAC

The sky all around Earth is divided into 88 constellations. The Sun and planets pass through only 12 of them. These 12 constellations are known as the zodiac.

SPOTLIGHT ON SPACE

One of the oldest constellations is Capricorn, the sea-goat.

CLOSE NEIGHBORS... OR NOT?

The stars in a constellation look close together, but mostly they are not. Some of them are much further away from us than others.

The furthest star in the constellation of Orion is five times further away than the closest star.

GALAXIES

Stars travel through space with other stars in giant groups called galaxies. The stars in a galaxy are held together by gravity, the same force that holds you down on the ground.

SPINNING IN SPACE

All the galaxies we can see are spinning as they travel through space. A big galaxy can take hundreds of millions of years to spin around once.

The Andromeda galaxy is a giant spinning disk of a trillion stars.

Spiral galaxies have long arms of stars curling out from the middle.

COUNTING GALAXIES

How many galaxies could there be in the whole Universe? Scientists have tried to figure this out. They think there are 100-200 billion galaxies!

SHAPES

There are three main types of galaxies. Some are spiral in shape. Others are elliptical, like a squashed ball. The rest have no clear shape. These are irregular galaxies.

THE MILKY WAY

We live in a galaxy called the Milky Way. It's a big spiral galaxy. The Sun is one of about 200 billion stars in the Milky Way.

OLD AND YOUNG

The Milky Way has a big ball of older stars in the middle, with a thin, flat disk of younger stars around it. The disk is made of long arms of stars.

THE LOCAL GROUP

The Milky Way moves through space with dozens of other galaxies. These galaxies are called the Local Group. The Milky Way is one of the biggest galaxies in the Local Group.

SPOTLIGHT ON SPACE

Older stars

Younger stars

The Milky Way is a flat, thin galaxy seen from the side.

You are here

The Sun is in one of the
Milky Way's star-filled arms.

SPINNING THROUGH SPACE

The Milky Way galaxy cartwheels through
space. The whole galaxy spins slowly. The Sun
takes about 225 million years to travel all the
way around the center of the galaxy.

CLOUDS IN SPACE

Galaxies contain giant clouds of gas and dust called nebulae. These clouds are cosmic nurseries where new stars are born.

LIGHT AND DARK

Some nebulae glow because they are lit up by nearby stars. Others are dustier and darker. They look like a dark shadow if there is a bright nebula behind them.

This dark cloud is called the Horsehead Nebula because of its shape.

SPOTLIGHT ON SPACE

MAKING NEBULAE

Stars are born in nebulae, but they can also make new nebulae. When a big star dies, it explodes. The explosion sprays gas and dust out into space, creating a nebula.

Fuzzy stars

Some stars end their days by pushing some
of their gas away into space. The gas looks
like a big fuzzy ball or ring around the star.
This is called a planetary nebula.

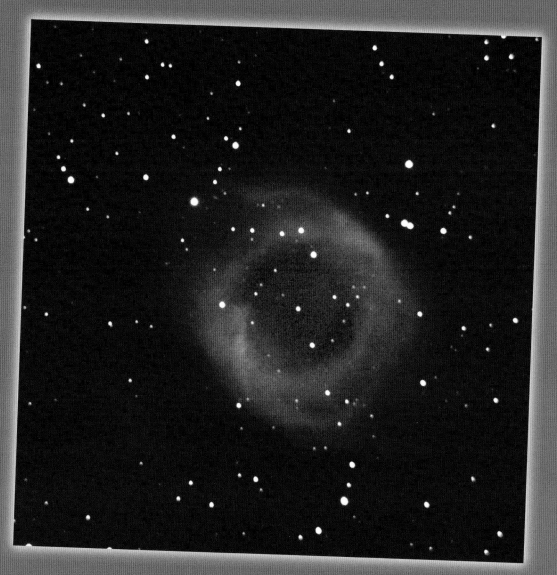

This star is surrounded by the
cloudy ring of a planetary nebula.

LOOKING AT STARS

The stars are so far away that we can't visit them or send spacecraft to explore them. Scientists study stars by using telescopes and other instruments on Earth.

TWINKLE, TWINKLE

Stars twinkle because starlight bends as it travels through air. Astronomers build telescopes on mountaintops, above most of the air. This reduces the twinkling, so astronomers can see the stars more clearly.

These telescopes are on top of Mauna Kea, a sleeping volcano in Hawaii.

RADIO PICTURES

Stars and galaxies give out radio waves as well as light. Radio telescopes receive these waves. Other types of telescopes work with other waves and rays, including X-rays and gamma rays.

SPOTLIGHT ON SPACE

SPACE TELESCOPES

Some telescopes are launched into space. There, they are above all the air and they can study all the light and other rays given out by stars and galaxies.

The Hubble Space Telescope orbits Earth 350 miles (560 km) above the ground.

HOW STARS DIE

After a few million or billion years, stars run out of the fuel they need to keep shining. Some stars fade away, but others explode.

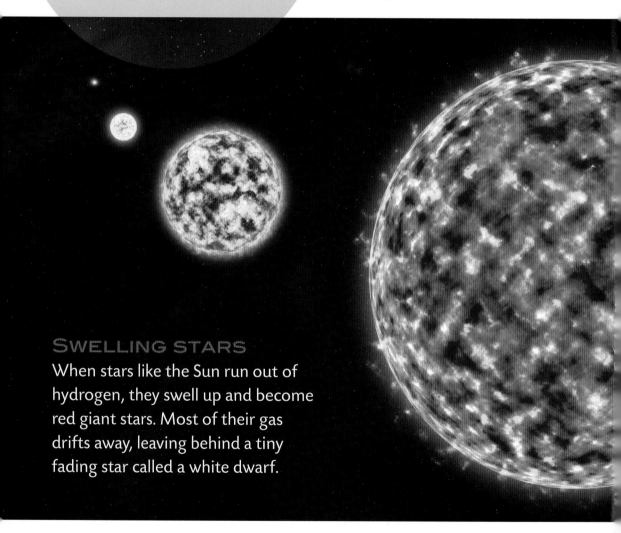

SWELLING STARS

When stars like the Sun run out of hydrogen, they swell up and become red giant stars. Most of their gas drifts away, leaving behind a tiny fading star called a white dwarf.

Stars turn red as they swell up, because their outer layers cool down.

FLASH! BANG!

Stars bigger than the Sun turn into red giants that tear themselves apart in a dazzling explosion called a supernova. A tiny dark star called a neutron star is left afterwards.

A supernova sends stardust flying in all directions.

HOLES IN SPACE

When a big star explodes, it makes a strange place called a black hole. The pull of gravity in a black hole is so amazingly strong that nothing can escape from it, not even light!

SPOTLIGHT ON SPACE

GLOSSARY

billion One thousand million.

black hole A place with such a strong pull of gravity that nothing can escape from it. Black holes are made when massive stars explode.

constellation One of the 88 groups of stars that include well-known patterns used by astronomers to find their way around the sky.

Earth The planet we live on. The third planet from the Sun.

galaxy Billions of stars and clouds of gas and dust traveling through space together, held together by gravity.

gravity A force that pulls everything towards a star, planet, moon or other large object.

legend A very old story that has been passed down from one generation to another for a long time.

Milky Way The galaxy we live in. It contains about 200 billion stars. One of them is the Sun.

myth An ancient story about heroes or monsters.

nebula A giant cloud of gas and dust in a galaxy.

neutron star A small dark star made of particles called neutrons, created when a big star explodes.

red giant A huge star that has swollen up as it begins to run out of the hydrogen that keeps it shining.

star A gigantic ball of glowing gas in space, giving out heat and light that are made in the center of the star.

Sun The closest star to Earth.

trillion One million million.

variable star A star that changes in brightness, growing brighter and then dimmer.

white dwarf A small, dim, fading star left behind when a small star such as the Sun has run out of fuel and lost most of its gas.

WEB SITES

http://starchild.gsfc.nasa.gov/docs/StarChild/universe_level1/milky_way.html
Information about our galaxy, the Milky Way, from the American space agency, NASA.

http://hubblesite.org
Everything you ever wanted to know about the Hubble Space Telescope and its discoveries.

http://spaceplace.nasa.gov/story-superstar/en/
An animated book about the Earth and Sun from the American space agency NASA.

http://www.sciencekids.co.nz/sciencefacts/space/sun.html
Learn how hot the Sun is, what it's made of and lots more Sun facts.

http://www.esa.int/esaKIDSen/SEM346WJD1E_OurUniverse_0.html
Lots of information about stars and galaxies from the European Space Agency.

http://scienceforkids.kidipede.com/physics/space/galaxy.htm
Galaxies, how many stars they have and how many galaxies there are.

http://bbc.co.uk/science/space/universe/sights/supernovae
Find out what a supernova is and why it happens.

http://www.kidsastronomy.com/black_hole.htm
Read more about black holes here.

INDEX